This book is arranged geographically from south to north. The index book region with page numbers for ease of reference.

Region: Campbeltown: Springbank (P8/9)

Region: Islay: Ardbeg (P10/11); Bowmore (P16); Bruichladdich (P18/19); Bunnahabhain (P22/23); Caol Ila (P20/21); Kilchoman (P17); Lagavulin (P12/13); Laphroaig (P14/15)

Region: Lowland: Glenkinchie (P26/27)

Region: Highland: Ben Nevis (P42/43); Blair Athol (P40/41); Clynelish (P90/91); Dalwhinnie (P44/45); Dewar's Aberfeldy Distillery (P38/39); Deanston (P30/31); Fettercairn (P48/49); Glen Garioch (P50/51); Glen Ord (P84/85 and P96); GlenDronach (P52/53); Glengoyne (P28/29); Glenmorangie (P88/89); Glenturret - The Famous Grouse (P5 and P32/33); Highland Park (P94/95); Jura (P24/25); Oban (P34/35); Pulteney (P92/93); Royal Lochnagar (P2-3 and P46/47); Talisker (P56/57); The Dalmore (P86/87); Tobermory (P36/37); Tomatin (P54/55)

Region: Speyside: Aberlour (P66/67); Balvenie (back cover); Benromach (P80/81); Cardhu (P64/65); Cragganmore (P60/61); Dallas Dhu (P82/83); Glen Grant (P74/75); Glenfarclas (P62/63); Glenfiddich (P72/73); Glen Moray (P78/79); Speyside Cooperage (P70/71); Strathisla (P7and P76/77); The Glenlivet (P1, P6 and P58/59); The Macallan (P68/69)

DISTINGUISHED
DISTILLERIES

NESS PUBLISHING

2 Royal Lochnagar Distillery, Royal Deeside.

DISTINGUISHED DISTILLERIES

Welcome to the world of whisky!

Whisky, especially Malt Whisky, stirs many emotions and memories. It is not just the whisky, but who you are enjoying it with, and perhaps the place, which engenders that special camaraderie. Whisky is a very social drink that encourages you to appreciate its many complexities and characteristics. We enjoy whisky to celebrate births, marriages and often at funerals where the departed has prescribed his or her favourite dram to be enjoyed after the ceremony. I was first introduced to whisky at a sporting occasion; my memory does not allow me to recollect whether I was celebrating or commiserating ... but that's part of the enjoyment! Whisky has a canny character that makes it appropriate at any event.

Scotland's distilleries are an integral part of the country's history and an engine of its economy. This book takes you on an illustrated tour of 44 of the most notable distilleries, from Campbeltown in the south-west to Orkney in the far north, with many mainland establishments in between. It is created both for the armchair traveller and for those touring Scotland with the particular aim of visiting the many distilleries that welcome visitors. Each one will tell you its stories and share its secrets. Each presentation is unique but each one shares its passion for the 'water of life'.

The Famous Grouse at Glenturret Distillery.   5

Enjoying Whisky

The most important way is your way! But I would encourage you to experiment with a little water; you decide whether it is a splash or a drop. A little water is an important means of helping you to appreciate fully the whisky you are drinking. It opens the whisky up and allows your taste buds to do their job and to distinguish the many flavours each whisky can deliver.

There are five different whisky producing regions in Scotland: Highland, Lowland, Speyside, Islay and Campbeltown. Although there are variations within each region, for the most part there is an underlying 'signature' taste and style to the whiskies produced in each one. Speyside is located within the Highland region and therefore whiskies produced there can be labelled as either Highland or Speyside.

The boundary that defines where the Lowlands end and the Highlands begin is known as the 'Highland Line'. It runs between the Clyde and Tay rivers (approximately from Perth to Greenock). Broadly speaking, everywhere to the north of this line is classed as Highland, although the exact course of the line has varied down the years. The origins of the Highland

6   In the new Still House at The Glenlivet Distillery.

Line go back to the 17th century when it was intended to help reduce tax evasion in the remoter parts of Scotland, where most whisky distilling was carried out illicitly and on which, therefore, no tax was paid. This meant that distilleries in the Lowlands bore the brunt of the tax burden. In an attempt to 'level the playing field', an Act of Parliament in 1784 imposed different rates of tax on each side of the line, with a lower tariff for the Lowland distillers. This then influenced where some distilleries were built and is thus part of the story of some of the distilleries we shall visit.

Scotland exports whisky to all corners of the world so you can enjoy a little bit of Scotland anywhere from Adelaide to Zurich. So wherever you are, slàinte mhath!

Finally, a gentle reminder that drinking and driving should never be encouraged while touring distilleries, so please have a dedicated driver while touring and tasting. Or better still, employ the services of a driver-guide so you can all immerse yourselves in the search for your favourite malt.

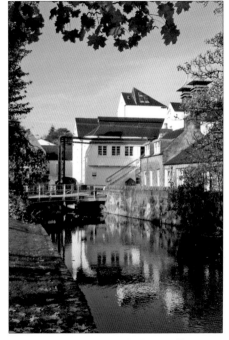

The River Isla flows through Strathisla Distillery. 7

Springbank (J&A Mitchell & Co. Ltd)

Region: Campbeltown

Tel No: 01586 552009

Address: Well Close, Campbeltown, Argyll, PA28 6ET

Web Address: www.springbankwhisky.com

Located on the Kintyre peninsula in Campbeltown, Springbank Distillery stands proudly in the centre of what used to be the whisky capital of Scotland: there was a time when 22 distilleries operated in the town. Springbank is unique in being the only distillery still independently owned by the same family since it first produced whisky legally. It is one of only a very few distilleries that carry out the entire process on site, from malting the barley to bottling the whisky. Springbank is also the only distillery in Scotland to produce three different whiskies, namely Springbank, Longrow and Hazelburn, all of which use different production techniques.

Colour, Nose and Tasting Notes:
Springbank 10 Year Old

Matured in Bourbon and Sherry oak casks, there are aromas of vanilla, hints of pear and on the palate rich spice of cinnamon, maltiness and more vanilla. The palate is lingering, sweetness from the pear and vanilla, with just a hint of the sea!

Each cask has to be stencilled before going into storage to be matured. 9

Ardbeg (Louis Vuitton Moet Hennessy)

Region: Islay

Tel No: 01496 302244

Address: Port Ellen, Isle of Islay, PA42 7EA

Web Address: www.ardbeg.com

Founded in 1815 by John MacDougall, Ardbeg has had a chequered history. Since reaching a production peak of 1.1 million litres of whisky in 1887, it has changed hands a few times and been closed twice. However, with current owners, The House of Glenmorangie and Moet Hennessey Louis Vuitton, by 2005 it had emulated the production quantities of 1887. The past few years have firmly established Ardbeg as an award-winning whisky with various expressions being awarded Whisky of the Year by the prestigious whisky writer Jim Murray. This includes the 10 Year Old Ardbeg Single Malt, the heart of the Ardbeg family.

Colour, Nose and Tasting Notes:
Ardbeg Corryvreckan

Ardbeg Corryvreckan is another award-winning whisky. The colour is gold with a hint of green. The nose has medicinal phenols, sitting alongside clementine and pineapple and a soft vanilla creaminess. The palate is enticed by plums and peach, the peat smoke is present but not powerful, leaving a peppery, salty savoury finish that is quite extraordinary.

Ardbeg Distillery.

Lagavulin (Diageo)

Region: Islay

Tel No: 01496 302749

Address: Port Ellen, Isle of Islay, PA42 7DZ

Web Address: www.discovering-distilleries.com

In 1816 John Johnston, a local farmer and distiller, founded Lagavulin Distillery. With the abundance of peat bogs on the west of the island, Lagavulin became famous for its heavily peated barley aromas. With a longer than average distillation process and with the most popular bottling of Lagavulin being the 16 Year Old, it is said that this enhances the aromas and flavours. Lagavulin is a long established classic from Islay which has the peat, the sea and the smoke all beautifully balanced in a great whisky.

Colour, Nose and Tasting Notes:
Lagavulin 16 Year Old

A deep amber gold colour and the nose is rich with smoke aromas infused with seaweed and hints of medicinal iodine. The peaty taste leads to the sea saltiness of smoked fish with sweetness from dried fruit. A complex whisky to savour at leisure.

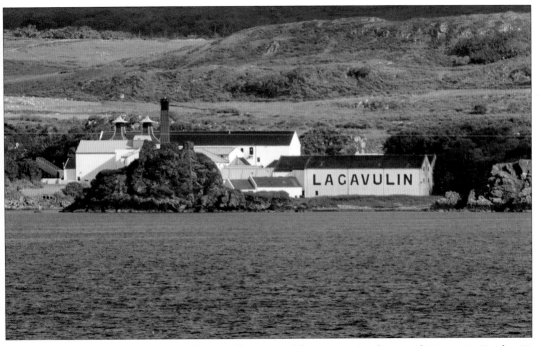

Lagavulin Distillery viewed from a passing ferry, with Dunyvaig Castle 13
on the rock in front of the chimney.

Laphroaig (D Johnston & Company (Laphroaig) Ltd)

Region: Islay

Tel No: 01496 302418

Address: Port Ellen, Isle of Islay, PA42 7DU

Web Address: www.laphroaig.com

This is the smokiest and most phenolic of all the Islay whiskies. Laphroaig translates to mean beautiful hollow by the broad bay. Founded in 1810 by the brothers Alexander and Donald Johnston, it officially started producing in 1815, reportedly after the excise men became suspicious! Because of its pungent aroma and smoky flavour, Laphroaig is an acquired taste loved by many. This is a whisky with eminent followers including Prince Charles, Duke of Rothesay, who gave his Royal Warrant to Laphroaig in 1994.

Colour, Nose and Tasting Notes:
Laphroaig Quarter Cask

Honey gold in colour, this young whisky provides aromas of peat smoke and TCP with a gentle sweetness of dried fruits. The palate finds chilli and peppers for warmth leading to a surprisingly sweet fruitiness, with lingering smoke. The finish is one of dry, warm smoke with a vanilla cream.

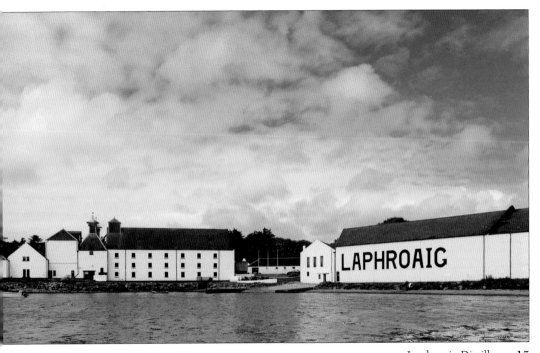

Laphroaig Distillery.

Bowmore (Beam Suntory)

Region: Islay

Tel No: 01496 810671

Address: School Street, Bowmore, Isle of Islay, PA43 7JS

Web Address: www.bowmore.com

This is the oldest distillery on Islay, founded in 1779. It is picturesquely located close to Bowmore harbour on Loch Indaal. Bowmore can be considered a rarity in that it still produces and malts up to 40% of its own barley. Most distillers buy in their malted barley from specialist maltsters.

Bowmore Distillery also matures most of its whisky in Sherry casks, which is unusual amongst the distillers on Islay, the majority of which use a mix of Sherry and American Bourbon casks.

Colour, Nose and Tasting Notes:

Bowmore Tempest 10 Year Old Batch 6

At the time of writing this is the latest release in the Tempest series. Aged for 10 years in ex- 1st fill bourbon casks, Batch 6 is rich gold in colour and has aromas of tropical fruits such as juicy clementine and sharp pineapple. The palate is alive with sweet nuttiness of almonds and soft peatiness. The finish is smooth vanilla with a gentle saltiness.

Kilchoman (Kilchoman Distillery Co Ltd)

Region: Islay   **Address:** Rockside Farm, Bruichladdich, Isle of Islay, PA49 7UT
Tel No: 01496 850011   **Web Address:** www.kilchomandistillery.com

Established in 2005, this is the first distillery to be constructed on Islay since 1908 and the smallest, producing just 100,000 litres per year. However, it has already won awards and is unique in that all the barley is grown on the farm adjacent to the distillery, where it is malted, distilled, matured and even bottled! In the last two years, Kilchoman has launched Machir Bay as its core expression. It releases a new batch each year and so far they have been very well received, each release demonstrating a consistent quality and developing flavours with maturation.

Colour, Nose and Tasting Notes:
Kilchoman Machir Bay 2015 Release

Pale gold colour. Nose: hints of oak rubbing with sweet meadow grass, tropical lemon with some sweet vanilla. Palate: red fruits at the forefront, then the peatiness kicks in with smokiness and sea salt warmth. Finish: medium length, spice, pepper, smooth, peaty.

Bruichladdich (Remy Cointreau)

Region: Islay

Tel No: 01496 850221

Address: Bruichladdich, Islay, Argyll, PA49 7UN

Web Address: www.bruichladdich.com

Like many distilleries, Bruichladdich has been owned by many companies since it was first constructed in 1881. At Bruichladdich they call themselves 'progressive Hebridean Distillers' and you cannot deny that they are! It is one of only two distilleries on Islay to bottle on the island. In 2002 it produced the most heavily peated whisky called Octomore and subsequently released such expressions as The Yellow Submarine, Rocks and Islay Barley 2007. Bruichladdich is also leading the way in converting waste from the distillery into electricity and can now power the distillery with electricity from the whisky waste! Naturally, as progressive as they are, they have a great organic whisky.

Colour, Nose and Tasting Notes:
Bruichladdich The Laddie Ten

Mid-gold in colour, bursting with tropical fruits, particularly lemon and sweet honey and oak aromas, and the palate livens with a richness of vanilla, honey, sweet spices and maltiness.

Bruichladdich Distillery. **19**

Caol Ila (Diageo)

Region: Islay

Tel No: 01496 302760

Address: Port Askaig, Isle of Islay, PA46 7RL

Web Address: www.discovering-distilleries.com

Located close to Port Askaig, Caol Ila (pronounced Cull Eela) is the largest distillery on Islay. For almost 100 years the whisky was taken by ship directly from the distillery to the mainland through the Sound of Islay – Caol Ila in Gaelic. Nowadays it is taken by lorry to the ferry and although there is warehousing at the distillery, much of the whisky is matured on the mainland. Caol Ila is a heavily peated, powerful whisky, typical of most Islay whiskies.

Colour, Nose and Tasting Notes:
Caol Ila 12 Year Old

Pale straw in colour, this whisky is full of peat smoke on the nose with hints of sea air, and a little almond. The palate is oily, slightly medicinal with smoke and some dried fruits.

Caol Ila Distillery. **21**

Bunnahabhain (Distell Ltd)

Region: Islay

Tel No: 01496 840646

Address: Port Askaig, Isle of Islay, PA46 7RP

Web Address: www.bunnahabhain.com & www.blackbottle.com

Built between 1881 and 1893 by the Greenlees brothers and now owned by Burn Stewart Distillers Ltd, Bunnahabhain Distillery is located at the northern end of Islay, reached by a single-track road which can make driving interesting if you meet a lorry coming towards you!

A considerable amount of the production goes into the famous blended Black Bottle Whisky. Unlike many of the Islay distilleries, Bunnahabhain does not have a hugely peaty aroma. This is because its water is piped directly from its limestone source and they do not use heavily peated barley. It is a soft, fruity malt, with a hint of the sea.

Colour, Nose and Tasting Notes:
Bunnahabhain 12 Year Old

Deep gold in colour, and a nose full of freshness with only a subtle reference to smoke, on the palate there are nutty and light fruit flavours with some malt and gentle smoke. The finish is quite short but pleasant.

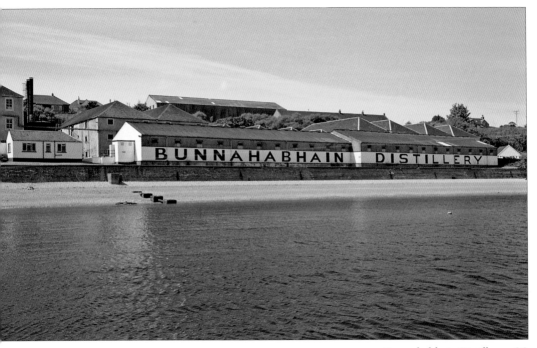

Bunnahabhain Distillery. **23**

Jura (Whyte & Mackay Ltd)

Region: Highland (Jura)

Tel No: 01496 820385

Address: Craighouse, Isle of Jura, Argyll, PA60 7XT

Web Address: www.jurawhisky.com

Established in 1810 by Archibald Campbell and located in the settlement of Craighouse (the main village on the island), it is only accessible via the neighbouring island of Islay. Jura whisky is known as the 'Highland from the Island'. It is very different from the whiskies produced on Islay as much less peat, if any, is used in most of the production. Owned by Whyte & Mackay, it went through a transformation when it was decided to re-rack the whisky, as many of the casks in the warehouses were not up to standard. This change, along with Master Blender Richard Paterson's expert nose, led to the creation in recent years of several new expressions, all of which have been well received.

Colour, Nose and Tasting Notes:
Isle of Jura Superstition

Rich orange-gold in colour. The nose experiences aromas of light peat smoke, spring blossom, toffee and hints of pepper. On the palate it is slightly oily; there are oats with toffee and honey sweetness. The finish is a medium length with the honey and pepper still present.

Isle of Jura Distillery. **25**

Glenkinchie (Diageo)

Region: Lowland

Tel No: 01875 342004

Address: Pencaitland, Tranent, East Lothian, EH34 5ET

Web Address: www.discovering-distilleries.com

Glenkinchie, also known as Edinburgh's distillery, is one of only five Lowland distilleries left in production. Although Lowland whisky is not as well known as some of the Highland and Speyside distilleries, the region was once at the heart of the whisky industry: in 1837 there were 115 distilleries in the Lowlands. Lowland whisky had the advantage of better roads and links to the north and south and also excellent agricultural land to ensure a plentiful supply of barley.

Colour, Nose and Tasting Notes:
Glenkinchie 12 Year Old

Mid gold in colour, Glenkinchie has light, grassy aromas that are fresh with hints of floral and smoke. It is dry on the palate, with plenty of malt and a long and dry finish.

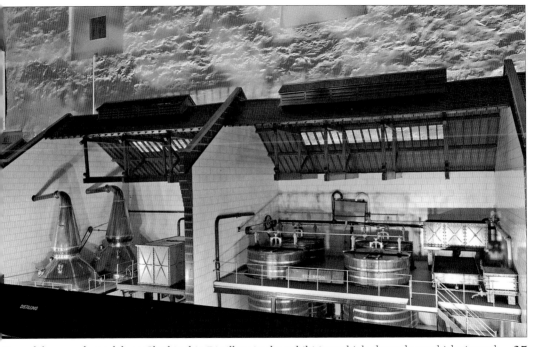

One of the superb models at Glenkinchie Distillery in the exhibition which shows how whisky is made. **27**

Glengoyne (Ian MacLeod Distillers Ltd)

Region: Southern Highlands

Address: Dumgoyne, Nr Killearn, Glasgow, G63 9LB

Tel No: 01360 550254

Web Address: www.glengoyne.com

Glengoyne Distillery is a very pretty distillery in the southern highlands, north of Glasgow. It takes its name from Glen Guin, meaning Glen of the Wild Geese. It has been in continuous production since 1833 and has always remained owned by Scottish Companies. Today it is owned by Ian Macleod Distillers Limited and carries a Royal Warrant. Intriguingly, the Highland Line is drawn such that Glengoyne Distillery is split in two, with the result that the whisky is produced in the Highlands but matured in the Lowlands!

Colour, Nose and Tasting Notes:

Glengoyne 15 Year Old

A warm, bright gold colour. The nose holds aromas of citrus lemon combined with a toffee sweetness and touches of cereal and oak. The palate experiences rich notes of butterscotch, nutty walnuts with hints of delicious cinnamon and just a little oiliness. The finish is dry with an oak and creamy malt.

Glengoyne Distillery. **29**

Deanston (Distell Ltd)

Region: Highland   Address: Deanston Distillery, Nr Doune, Stirling District, FK16 6AG

Tel No: 01786 843010   Web Address: www.deanstonmalt.com

Deanston stands alongside the waters of the River Teith near the small town of Doune. It is a relatively young distillery, founded in the mid 1960s when it took over the premises of a former cotton mill. Whisky production began in 1966. Then owned by James Finlay & Co and Brodie Hepburn, it has changed hands a few times over the years and is now owned by Burn Stewart Distillers. They re-branded Deanston as a single malt in 2009, increasing the ABV from 40% to 46.3% on the 12 Year Old un-chill filtered single malt. They have also released various limited editions that have proved so popular that they are challenging to find. A visit to the distillery is highly recommended to sample Deanston Spanish Oak and Deanston Toasted Oak.

Colour, Nose and Tasting Notes:

Deanston 12 Year Old un-chill filtered

Bright golden colour, fresh cereal and malt aromas with hints of fragrant heather and oak. The palate is awakened with spices including ginger and cloves with orange leading to a satisfying fruity finish with lingering spice.

Deanston Distillery. **31**

Glenturret - The Famous Grouse Experience (Edrington)

Region: Eastern Highlands   **Address: The Hosh, Crieff, Perthshire, PH7 4HA**

Tel No: 01764 656565   **Web Address:** www.thefamousgrouse.com

Arguably the oldest distillery in Scotland, Glenturret Distillery can be dated back to 1775 when whisky smugglers created a small, illicit still. Glenturret, formerly known as Hosh Distillery, is the established home of the Famous Grouse blended whisky and welcomes tens of thousands of visitors every year. Most of the whisky produced is used for blending and Famous Grouse is the top-selling blended whisky in Scotland. Originally named 'Grouse' in 1896 by Perthshire merchant Matthew Gloag, who added the word 'Famous' in 1905 following the enormous popularity of the blend he had created. There are a few limited bottlings of single malt, notably the 10 Year Old. Glenturret is also famous for its cat Towser, who made it in to the Guinness Book of Records for killing 28,899 mice. She lived for 24 years and only the kills found near the stills were counted. Her other victims included pheasants and rabbits!

Colour, Nose and Tasting Notes:
The Glenturret 10 Year Old

Pale amber in colour, on the nose it is fresh, fruity and with aromas of barley. The palate is fruity with a hint of nuts with some honey sweetness. Not a long finish, but a very pleasant classic malt.

32

Glenturret Distillery, home of the Famous Grouse. 33

Located in the centre of the west highland town of the same name, Oban Distillery is said to have been in existence before the town and that the town grew around it. It certainly sits in the heart of Oban and therefore there is no opportunity to expand, with buildings on three sides and a steep rock face on the other. Close to the harbour and looking over towards the Isle of Mull, Oban Distillery has just two stills which limits production, but this small distillery produces quality whisky that is used only for single malts, the 14 Year Old being one of the most popular.

Colour, Nose and Tasting Notes:
Oban 14 Year Old

Rich gold in colour, with coastal sea-salt aromas, light peat and some honey notes. The taste is well rounded with some toffee, sherried oak, autumn fruits, some more peat smoke and the finish is long and smooth.

Oban Distillery.

Tobermory (Distell Ltd)

Region: Highland (Mull)
Tel No: 01688 302647

Address: Tobermory, Isle of Mull, PA75 6NR
Web Address: www.tobermorymalt.com

Started in 1798 by John Sinclair, Tobermory Distillery was owned for a short time by the same company that owned Oban Distillery. Over the last 200 years it has spent many years closed, either through bankruptcy or refurbishment. Located close to the harbour in the picturesque town of Tobermory, it is now producing two very different whiskies. Tobermory is distilled from unpeated barley, very unusual for an island whisky, and matured for a minimum of 10 years. Ledaig, distilled from peated barley, is cut from the spirit still at a lower alcohol content to retain the powerful peaty flavours.

Colour, Nose and Tasting Notes:
Ledaig 10 Year Old

Pale straw in colour, this is the peated single malt from Tobermory Distillery. The nose invokes the sea breeze of the island alongside gentle peat smoke. The palate discovers pepper, raisins and figs with hints of vanilla oak and more gentle smoke. The finish is of medium length, a little smoke and spice.

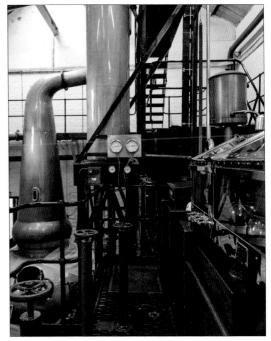

Left: part of the exterior of Tobermory Distillery. Right: inside the Still House at Tobermory Distillery. **37**

Dewar's Aberfeldy Distillery (Bacardi Limited)

Region: Eastern Highlands

Tel No: 01887 822010

Address: Aberfeldy, Perthshire, PH15 2EB

Web Address: www.dewars.com

Located on the edge of the picturesque town of Aberfeldy and close to the River Tay, this distillery was founded by John and Tommy Dewar in 1896. They were following in their father's footsteps, who had set up his own spirits business and knew that money could be made from whisky, having been blending and selling his own successfully for many years. In order to continue to produce and ensure the quality of their best-selling Dewar's White Label, they built Aberfeldy Distillery which to this day provides the base malt for this famous blend.

Colour, Nose and Tasting Notes:
Aberfeldy 12 Year Old

The colour is amber and the nose is rich and rounded with aromas of cereal, heather honey, slightly smoky, with hints of toffee. The palate is warmed with flavours of honey, spices and citrus. The finish is long and drying.

Dewar's Aberfeldy Distillery. The distillery used to operate its own steam shunting locomotive back **39** when Aberfeldy was on the rail network. It can be seen on the left.

Blair Athol (Diageo)

Region: Eastern Highlands

Tel No: 01796 482003

Address: Pitlochry, Perthshire, PH16 5LY

Web Address: www.discovering-distilleries.com

The first known distillery on this site was in 1798 when John Stewart and Robert Robertson built a distillery here called Aldour, named after the Allt Dour burn meaning 'burn of the otter'. When the First World War broke out, the men working at the distillery were sent off to war with a free bottle and the women continued to make the whisky. However, when prohibition was imposed in the USA, trade disappeared and the distillery closed. In 1933 it was bought by Arthur Bell and Son, although it remained closed during the Second World War. It re-opened in 1945 and has been in production ever since. It has always been used as part of the Bell's blend since the 1850s when Arthur Bell would travel around distilleries experimenting with blending.

Colour, Nose and Tasting Notes:
Blair Athol 12 Year Old

The colour is a rich amber and the nose is mellow with Sherry, spice and citrus fruit. The palate is full bodied, with dried fruits, citrus and a sweetness of caramel. The finish is warming and long.

Blair Athol Distillery, flying the flag for Bell's. **41**

Ben Nevis (Ben Nevis Distillery (Fort William) Ltd)

Region: Western Highlands

Tel No: 01397 700200

Address: Lochy Bridge, Fort William, PH33 6TJ

Web Address: www.bennevisdistillery.com

Lying at the foot of Britain's highest mountain, Ben Nevis, on the outskirts of Fort William, it was established in 1825 by John Macdonald. It draws its water from the Allt a' Mhuilinn which originates from two pools high up the mountain. The distillery has had a chequered history, having been closed twice, but has gone from strength to strength since being acquired in 1989 by Nikka Distilling Company from Japan. As well as producing a single malt, its whisky also forms an integral part in the blended Dew of Ben Nevis.

Colour, Nose and Tasting Notes:
Ben Nevis 10 Year Old

Pale amber in colour, on the nose there are subtle hints of orange and smoky peatiness. The palate is full with the complexities of toffee, hints of chocolate, oak and as it lingers, fruity notes appear. The finish is long, pleasant and malty.

Ben Nevis Distillery, with 'The Ben' itself rising up behind. **43**

Dalwhinnie (Diageo)

Region: Northern Highlands
Tel No: 01540 672219

Address: Dalwhinnie, Inverness-shire, PH19 1AF
Web Address: www.discovering-distilleries.com

The name Dalwhinnie comes from the Gaelic for a 'meeting place' for cattle and sheep drovers. The mountains that surround Dalwhinnie Distillery are both dramatic and beautiful: this is where the Cairngorms meet the Monadhliath Mountains and where you will find Scotland's second-highest distillery, Dalwhinnie. Founded in 1897 and originally called Strathspey, one can only hazard a guess as to why such a wild and windswept location was chosen for a whisky distillery. However, as well as having an ample supply of spring water, its remoteness was lessened by locating it alongside the Highland Railway line, which offered a safe and regular distribution link to get the whisky to market.

Colour, Nose and Tasting Notes:
Dalwhinnie 1997 (Bottled 2014)

Warm amber in colour. The nose has rich dried fruits from the Oloroso casks and light peat. The palate welcomes warm rich raisins and plums, cloves and cinnamon spices and a refined maltiness. The finish is dry and lingers with vanilla, oak and warming peat.

Dalwhinnie Distillery at night.

Royal Lochnagar (Diageo)

Region: Eastern Highlands

Tel No: 01339 742700

Address: Crathie, Ballater, Aberdeenshire, AB35 5TB

Web Address: www.discovering-distilleries.com

Originally named Lochnagar, it was founded in 1823 by James Robertson at a time when the Lochnagar mountains were still home to many whisky smugglers. The distillery was burnt down twice between 1826 and 1841. However, it benefited from Queen Victoria and Prince Albert's purchase of the adjacent Balmoral Castle. Following a visit to the distillery by the Royal couple, Lochnagar became an official supplier to the Crown and therefore could add the 'Royal' prefix to its name.

Colour, Nose and Tasting Notes:
Royal Lochnagar 12 Year Old

Rich old gold colour, a whisper of toffee and woody notes on the nose. The palate has flavours of malty sweetness, Sherry and a hint of smoke. Good balance with a medium finish.

Royal Lochnagar Distillery.

Fettercairn (Whyte & Mackay Ltd)

Region: Highland

Tel No: 01561 340244

Address: Fettercairn, Laurencekirk, Aberdeenshire, AB30 1YB

Web Address: www.fettercairndistillery.co.uk

The picturesque village of Fettercairn nestles in the foothills of the eastern Cairngorms. Its distillery is one of Scotland's oldest. Originally run by tenant farmers, whisky was produced in its current location from 1824 by Sir Alexander Ramsay, owner of Fasque Estate. It was later sold to Sir John Gladstone, father of Victorian Prime Minister William Gladstone, who was responsible for legalising the sale of bottled whisky to the public and ending the punitive Malt Tax.

Owned by Whyte & Mackay since the 1970s, Fettercairn has a reputation for producing light, well-structured whisky. Only 4% of the whisky produced is bottled as single malt, the rest being used for blends of Whyte & Mackay.

Colour, Nose and Tasting Notes:

Fettercairn Fior

Fior is Gaelic for 'true'. Released in 2010 and with no age statement, it is a remarkable whisky, packed with ripe fruits and Sherry on the nose with hints of dark chocolate. Smooth on the palate with more melted chocolate, combined with spiced cinnamon and nutmeg, hints of orange with a certain peatiness lingering. The finish is well rounded, drying in time with hints of oak and sweetness of butterscotch.

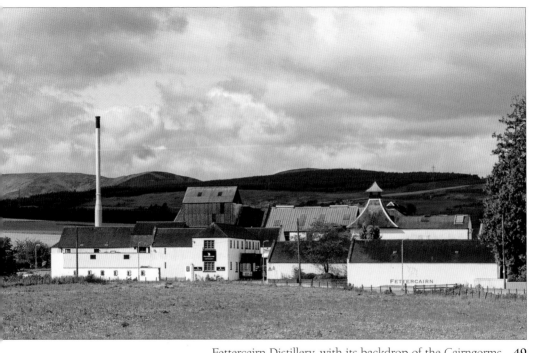

Fettercairn Distillery, with its backdrop of the Cairngorms. **49**

Glen Garioch (Beam Suntory)

Region: Eastern Highlands   **Address:** Distillery Road, Old Meldrum, Aberdeenshire, AB51 0ES

Tel No: 01651 873450   **Web Address:** www.glengarioch.com

John and Alexander Manson founded Glen Garioch Distillery in 1797. Pronounced Glen Geery, the distillery was located next to a brewery. The Manson brothers, like many new distillers, came from a farming family. John Manson and his wife Elizabeth's second son, Patrick, found recognition after graduating in medicine from Aberdeen University when he discovered a direct link between mosquitoes and malaria. Over the past two hundred years, Glen Garioch has been transferred to various owners and been closed due to a shortage of water. A new spring was subsequently found. In the 1970s, in response to escalating fuel costs, the owners developed a system of using waste heat from the distillery to power an acre of greenhouses and an acre of polytunnels to produce vegetables. Over the last few years the brand has been completely revamped and the 12 Year Old is matured in both Bourbon and Sherry casks.

Colour, Nose and Tasting Notes:
Glen Garioch Founder's Reserve

Rich mahogany in colour, dry and spicy on the nose with hints of orchard apples. The palate has a buttery sweetness with honey and oak. The finish is smooth and subtle.

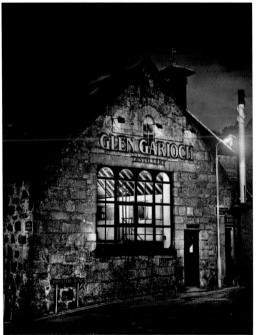

Two artistic views of Glen Garioch Distillery. **51**

GlenDronach (BenRiach Distillery Co)

Region: Highland
Tel No: 01466 730202

Address: Forgue, by Huntly, Aberdeenshire, AB54 6DB
Web Address: www.glendronachdistillery.co.uk

GlenDronnach Distillery is located just outside Speyside, near the town of Huntly. It has been producing whisky for nearly 200 years and at one point paid the most duty of any distillery in Scotland. Some forty years ago it was one of the top five selling single malts in the world. It has always had a loyal following and reputation for heavily sherried whisky. The distillery is unique in that its mash tun is made from copper, something no longer seen in distilleries, but once traditional. Since it was purchased by BenRiach Distillery Company in 2008 it has benefited from major investment and has won accolades for its whisky across the globe.

Colour, Nose and Tasting Notes:
GlenDronach 15 Year Old Revival

Rich gold from being matured entirely in Oloroso casks, strong aromas of Sherry and orange fruit. Flavours of Christmas pudding, spices of nutmeg, cinnamon and influences of toffee with a lengthy finish to savour.

GlenDronach Distillery. **53**

Tomatin (Tomatin Distillery Co Ltd)

Region: Highland
Tel No: 01463 248144

Address: Tomatin, Inverness-shire, IV13 7YT
Web Address: www.tomatin.com

Started by a group of Inverness businessmen during the whisky boom of the late 1800s, Tomatin Distillery is on the eastern edge of the Monadhliath Mountains. It is located on an old drovers' trail and can date selling illegal whisky back to the 15th century when drovers would fill a flask from a still at the Old Laird's House. Tomatin was once the largest distillery in Scotland, having grown rapidly in the 1960s and 70s when production reached 12 million litres of alcohol. It is also unusual in that it employs its own coopers to repair casks, and many of the families who work at the distillery also live in houses provided for them. Tomatin is a real community whisky.

Colour, Nose and Tasting Notes:

Tomatin 14 Year Old Port Wood Finish

A rose-tinted gold colour, powerful aromas of toffee and baked apples. The palate is packed with red berry fruitiness and juicy raisins. There is bitter dark chocolate, vanilla and oak are present with hints of white pepper. The finish is very fruity, nutty, long and lingering.

Tomatin Distillery from the air.

Talisker (Diageo)

Region: Highlands (Skye)

Tel No: 01478 614308

Address: Carbost, Isle of Skye, IV47 8SR

Web Address: www.discovering-distilleries.com

Talisker is the only distillery on the Isle of Skye. It is protected from the stormy Atlantic Ocean by its sheltered location at Carbost near the head of Loch Harport. Built in 1830 by brothers Hugh and Kenneth MacAskill, it did not stay in their hands for very long before being taken over. Making it a viable business proved difficult, probably due to its location; matters were made worse when one owner's agent was imprisoned for selling casks that did not exist! Talisker was triple-distilled (spirit is normally distilled twice) until the late 1920s. In 1960 the Still House burnt down leaving it with no production for two years, but fortunately the warehouses remained untouched. Since Talisker 10 Year Old became part of Diageo's Classic Malt collection it has become very popular and the visitor centre welcomes over 50,000 visitors annually.

Colour, Nose and Tasting Notes:
Talisker Port Ruighe

Copper gold colour, light on the nose with rich honeycomb sweetness, some raisin and plum, a little oily. The palate is lively with rich plummy fruits, chocolate and cinder toffee combined with smoke. The finish is sweet malt biscuit with more smoke.

Talisker Distillery.

The Glenlivet (Chivas Brothers)

Region: Speyside   **Address: Glenlivet, Ballindalloch, Banffshire, AB37 9DB**

Tel No: 01340 821720   **Web Address:** www.theglenlivet.com & www.maltwhiskydistilleries.com

A farmer by the name of George Smith (see picture on p.4) founded Glenlivet in 1824 in one of Speyside's remotest glens. It has a fascinating story that tells of heroic acts. George Smith carried pistols to protect himself from the smugglers who resented his pioneering shift from illicit to licensed distiller. His whisky was considered the very best, even being asked for by name by King George IV on his state visit to Edinburgh in 1822. Other distilleries tried to copy and added the name 'Glenlivet' to their own whisky in an effort to signify that theirs too was whisky of very high quality. After much legal wrangling over many years, owner John Gordon Smith won the case and there is now only one whisky worthy of the name The Glenlivet.

Colour, Nose and Tasting Notes:
The Glenlivet 21 Year Old Archive

Rich mahogany in colour. The nose offers aromas of Christmas pudding, ripe raisins, cinnamon and spice. The palate denotes the heavily sherried casks, with a nuttiness, rich spices and creamy toffee. The finish is sweet and warm with hints of oak.

The Glenlivet Distillery.

Cragganmore (Diageo)

Region: Speyside
Tel No: 01479 874715

Address: Ballindalloch, Banffshire, AB37 9AB
Web Address: www.discovering-distilleries.com

Cragganmore distillery nestles in a pretty glen in the heart of Speyside close to Ballindalloch Castle. It was founded in 1869 by the very experienced John Smith, who had previously run Glenfarclas and Ballindalloch distilleries. The first 'whisky special' train ran from Ballindalloch in 1887 for Aberdeen with 25 wagons carrying 300 casks of Cragganmore. In the 1920s it was partly owned by Ballindalloch Estate. Cragganmore has set itself apart from others by having very unusual flat-topped stills which, along with the worm tubs that cool the vapours, all help to create a complex whisky that is very aromatic. Most of its production is sent for blending and it is used in the White Horse blend amongst others.

Colour, Nose and Tasting Notes:
Cragganmore 12 Year Old

Straw gold in appearance with floral and herb aromas on the nose, it is a dry whisky with woody, maltiness notes and some orange fruit. There is a little smoke and peat on the finish.

Whisky maturing at Cragganmore Distillery.

Glenfarclas (J & G Grant)

Region: Speyside
Tel No: 01807 500257

Address: Ballindalloch, Banffshire, AB37 9BD
Web Address: www.glenfarclas.co.uk

Founded in 1836 by Robert Hay, bought in 1865 by the Grant Family and now being run by the sixth generation of the family, Glenfarclas has a renowned reputation for excellence of quality. While most production is concentrated on producing single malt, it is much sought after by blenders for its consistent quality. In 1968 Glenfarclas was also the first to introduce a cask-strength whisky. Latterly named Glenfarclas 105, it was ahead of its time as it was thought that there would not be a market for a cask-strength single malt. Glenfarclas also led the way in being one of the first to create a visitor centre.

Colour, Nose and Tasting Notes:
Glenfarclas 10 Year Old

Warm amber in colour, there is plenty of sherried fruit on the nose, ripe raisin and cinnamon-baked apples combine with heather-honey sweetness. On the palate there are winter spiced fruits, butterscotch and hints of nuttiness. The finish is fruity and spicy.

Left: a retired still makes a striking feature at Glenfarclas Distillery. Right: the Visitor Centre. **63**

Cardhu (Diageo)

Region: Speyside
Tel No: 01479 874635

Address: Knockando, Moray, AB38 7RY
Web Address: www.discovering-distilleries.com

Cardhu was started in 1824 by John Cummings, a former whisky smuggler whose original distillery was sited higher up on the Mannoch Hill. The distillery was mainly run by his wife, Helen, who would sell the whisky from the farm house. It moved to the existing site in 1885 and was operated as a farm distillery using its own barley. By this time it was being managed by Helen's daughter-in-law, Elizabeth – women's involvement in whisky production was very unusual at this time. When the new distillery was built, the old stills were sold to William Grant who used them to found Glenfiddich Distillery. Over the years, as production increased, more of Cardhu's high quality single malt was purchased by Johnnie Walker & Sons to be used in their blends. In 1893 Elizabeth sold the distillery to Johnnie Walker & Sons and it is now the established home of Johnnie Walker blended whisky, although Cardhu continues to produce a single malt.

Colour, Nose and Tasting Notes:
Cardhu 12 Year Old

Pale straw in colour with light, floral notes, hints of orchard pears, a malty nutty palate with sweetness of toffee and a small amount of peat. A medium length of finish that is crisp.

Cardhu Distillery, set amongst the barley fields that historically have provided **65** this raw material for its whisky.

Aberlour (Chivas Brothers)

Region: Speyside

Tel No: 01340 881249

Address: High Street, Aberlour, Banffshire, AB38 9PJ

Web Address: www.aberlour.com

Aberlour Distillery sits in the heart of Speyside, arguably Scotland's finest whisky-making area. Two thirds of all the producing distilleries are located around Speyside. A distillery was built in Aberlour in 1826, shortly after the first licences were issued. However, it was destroyed by fire and when rebuilt under the ownership of grain merchant James Fleming, it was moved to the other end of the village to its present location. Aberlour is Gaelic for mouth of the chattering burn. James Fleming was a man who worked hard at putting something back in to the community that had served him so well and financed the construction of the Aberlour Town Hall, the Cottage Hospital and the Penny Bridge. Aberlour also 'double casks' most of its whisky. This means some is matured in Sherry butts and some in Bourbon casks before being married together to produce an excellent Speyside Single Malt.

Colour, Nose and Tasting Notes:
Aberlour 18 Year Old

A deep, rich amber gold colour. The nose is creamy with vanilla, rich fruit and honey. To taste, your mouth senses fresh orchard apples and ripe orange alongside rich sherry and even more vanilla. The finish is complex with plummy sultanas, raisins and smooth butterscotch.

The Gatehouse at Aberlour Distillery. **67**

The Macallan (The Edrington Group)

Region: Speyside

Tel No: 01340 872280

Address: Craigellachie, Aberlour, AB38 9RX

Web Address: www.themacallan.com

The Macallan Distillery sits high above the River Spey with majestic views across to Ben Rinnes. Like some other distilleries on Speyside, it was founded by a farmer, Alexander Reid, who leased the land from the Earl of Seafield. It is thought that the Macallan name comes from two Gaelic words, 'Magh' meaning fertile piece of ground and 'Ellan' meaning 'of St Fillan', an Irish-born monk who evangelized Scotland in the eighth century. Macallan has always produced whisky of exceptional quality, ensuring all their casks are imported from Jerez in Spain after first being used for Oloroso Sherry, making it one of the most popular single malts globally.

Colour, Nose and Tasting Notes:
The Macallan Gold

Clear bright gold in colour, the nose has citrus fruit of lemon and orange, combined with hints of fresh green apple and sweet vanilla. The palate has sweet vanilla, a gentle oak, baked apple and citrus still present. The finish is dry, with some spice and oak.

The Macallan Distillery sits on the hillside above the River Spey near Craigellachie. **69**
Ben Rinnes (840m/2755ft) is in the distance.

Without the cask there wouldn't be whisky as we know it today. Wines and spirits can only be matured in casks made from oak as it doesn't seep as much as other woods. Traditionally, the whisky industry uses either American Oak from Bourbon Casks or European Oak from Sherry or wine casks. The word 'cooper' comes from the Latin 'cupa', meaning vat, so coopering has been a trade since Roman times.

The family-owned and run Speyside Cooperage is where you can see how the casks used to mature whisky are produced. As the only working cooperage in the UK, this is a unique experience where you will learn about the craft of coopering and see how traditional methods are used to build, mend and char the casks. You can even try it for yourself! Many generations of the same family have been coopers, using tools with strange names that have been passed down from father to son. These casks can last a century, and the trees used to produce them may already be a hundred or more years old when cut. It is an art that is still very much in demand, and there is no machine that can take the place of man!

Thousands of casks carefully stacked at the Speyside Cooperage. In the distance, further down 71 Speyside, other aspects of the whisky industry can be seen.

Glenfiddich (William Grant & Sons Ltd)

Region: Speyside

Tel No: 01340 820373

Address: Dufftown, Banffshire, AB55 4DH

Web Address: www.glenfiddich.com

Glenfiddich is in Dufftown, the whisky capital of Speyside. Founded in 1886 by William Grant who had worked previously for Mortlach Distillery, learning the trade as a young boy and working his way up to become distillery manager. The first spirit ran from the stills at Glenfiddich Distillery on Christmas Day 1887 – it had taken William Grant and his family little over a year to construct a distillery. It is now the whisky with the most awards and once tasted, it's easy to understand why. Glenfiddich means 'Valley of the Deer', hence the impressive stag's head on the famous logo.

Colour, Nose and Tasting Notes:
The Glenfiddich 18 Year Old

Warm amber in colour, there are orchard fruits on the nose, entwined with plump raisins, cinnamon and ginger. The palate has a fusion of sticky toffee pudding sweetness with some oak, spice and toffee apples. The finish is long, spicy and fruity.

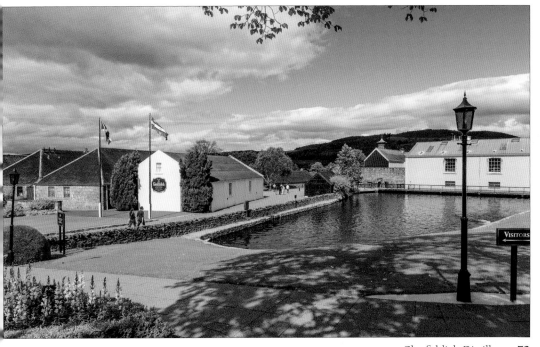

Glenfiddich Distillery.

Glen Grant (Campari Group)

Region: Speyside

Tel No: 01340 832118

Address: Rothes, Moray, AB38 7BS

Web Address: www.glengrant.com

Glen Grant distillery is located in the Speyside town of Rothes, where there are several distilleries. Founded in 1840 by brothers James and John Grant, who had previously managed Dandaleith Distillery. By 1897 the family had expanded the distillery and created a new one across the road that was named Glen Grant No.2, but sadly it was mothballed just five years later. It wasn't until 1965 that production restarted at Glen Grant No.2 and it was renamed Caperdonich. Since 1965 there have been several owners, including Chivas and Diageo. It is now owned by Campari and is a very popular single malt in Italy. Their most popular single malt is the 10 Year Old. In recent years they have focused on the American market.

Colour, Nose and Tasting Notes:
Glen Grant – The Major's Reserve

Light gold in colour. The nose has light citrus and green apple notes. The palate is light, apple fruit, softly creamy and the finish is dry with oak and a hint of toasted nuts. A great aperitif.

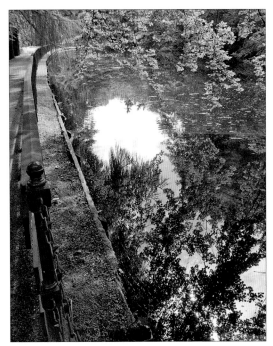

Glen Grant Distillery is famous for its fine gardens as well as its excellent whisky. **75**
Left: the burn (stream) that provides the distillery's water source. Right: the distillery pond.

Strathisla (Chivas Brothers)

Region: Speyside   Address: Seafield Avenue, Keith, Banffshire, AB55 5BS

Tel No: 01542 783044   Web Address: www.chivas.com & www.maltwhiskydistilleries.com

Arguably the prettiest distillery on Speyside, Strathisla is situated in the town of Keith. It is the spiritual home of Chivas Regal Blended Whisky and, as such, there is more emphasis on this than on the single malt of Strathisla. Founded in 1786, it has had a turbulent history that includes a major fire in 1876, followed some years later by an explosion and one owner being jailed for black market dealings which led to bankruptcy in 1949. Following the bankruptcy, the company that also owned Chivas Brothers acquired the distillery at auction in 1950 and have invested substantially since then. Alongside increasing the number of stills to boost output, the historic buildings have been restored and maintained to a high standard.

Colour, Nose and Tasting Notes:
The Strathisla 12 Year Old

Gold in colour with rich aromas of spice, plump raisins and malt. On the palate there are hints of toffee and oak, with Sherry definition and a little smoke.

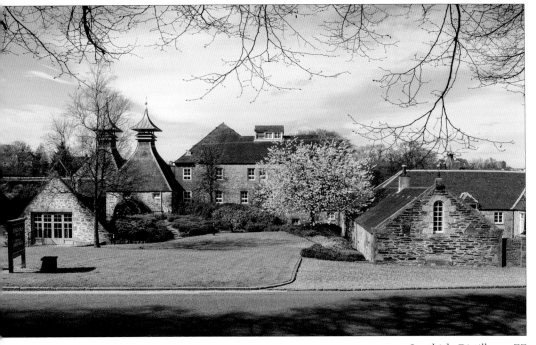

Strathisla Distillery.

Glen Moray (La Martiniquaise)

Region: Speyside

Tel No: 01343 550900

Address: Bruceland Road, Elgin, IV30 1YE

Web Address: www.glenmoray.com

Originally a brewery, Glen Moray has now been producing whisky for over 100 years. The main road to Elgin, reportedly travelled by St Columba, King Duncan and Bonnie Prince Charlie, used to pass through the distillery, which is located in the shadow of Gallow Hill where executions used to take place. Glen Moray uses Bourbon casks to mature the whisky although some are finished in Madeira, Chardonnay and Chenin Blanc casks to create different expressions.

Colour, Nose and Tasting Notes:
Glen Moray 12 Year Old

Mid gold in colour, with aromas of vanilla and malt and some pear fruit. The taste is smooth, balanced and rounded with flavours of vanilla, malt and some toffee, leading to a long pleasing finish.

The Still House at Glen Moray Distillery.

Benromach (Gordon & MacPhail)

Region: Speyside

Address: Invererne Road, Forres, Moray, IV36 3EB

Tel No: 01309 675968

Web Address: www.benromach.com

Benromach is the smallest distillery in Speyside. Bought by Gordon & MacPhail in 1993 from the much larger United Distillers, it has had a chequered life with the distillery being mothballed twice, once in 1931 and again in 1983. There are only two members of staff employed at the distillery and they produce approximately 150,000-250,000 litres of spirit per year. Benromach was the first distillery to produce an Organic Whisky fully certified by the Soil Association. Gordon & MacPhail is continually trying continually trying new and innovative ways of adding different expressions to the brand and have released whiskies from single barley varieties and also Madeira and Port Pipes finishes.

Colour, Nose and Tasting Notes:
The Benromach 10 Year Old

Rich gold in colour, with light smoke on the nose, hints of Sherry and creamy vanilla, subtle spices such as ginger on the palate with ripe raisins and a delicate smokiness, all beautifully balanced and with a good length of finish.

Benromach Distillery. **81**

Dallas Dhu (Historic Scotland)

Region: Speyside

Tel No: 01309 676548

Address: Forres, Moray, IV36 2RR

Web Address: www.historic-scotland.gov.uk

The name means Black Water Valley and it was built in 1898 to produce whisky for the Glasgow firm of Wright and Greigs. They had a blend called Roderick Dhu of which Dallas Dhu formed the basis. After going into liquidation in 1921 it was sold to Benmore Distillers, who used it in their blends; it was also bottled under the name of Dallas Mhor. Dallas Dhu ceased production in 1983 mainly due to a lack of water and has since become a museum. Independent bottlings of Dallas Dhu can still be purchased although with each year that passes these will gradually deplete.

Colour, Nose and Tasting Notes:

Roderick Dhu Blended Scotch Whisky

Very pale straw in colour with green hues. The nose has smoky overtones, this leads pleasantly on to the palate with a lingering finish. A very pleasant blend and works well as a dram on its own or with a mixer.

Dallas Dhu Historic Distillery, located just to the south of Forres. **83**

Glen Ord (Diageo)

Region: Northern Highlands
Tel No: 01463 872004

Address: Muir of Ord, Ross-shire, IV6 7UJ
Web Address: www.discovering-distilleries.com

Located in the village of Muir of Ord and close to the barley fields of the Black Isle, Glen Ord is one of the last surviving distilleries north-west of Inverness. It has changed hands many times since it was established in 1838 by Thomas Mackenzie. Today it belongs to global company Diageo for whom it plays an important role as it has a substantial maltings that supplies malted barley to many of their distilleries. During its history it has produced whisky under several names including Glen Oran and Glenordie, with the most recent being Singleton of Glen Ord. It is bottled at 12 years and sold exclusively to selected Asian markets, although it is available to buy at the distillery. Glen Ord also supplies whisky for famous blends such as Johnnie Walker.

Colour, Nose and Tasting Notes:

Glen Ord 25 Year Old 1990 (cask 10872) – Old Particular (Douglas Laing)

This is a rare bottling of Glen Ord from a single cask. Mid-gold in colour. On the nose it is light with floral notes, some lemon and subtle creamy toffee. In the mouth the citrus lemon is still present with hints of spiced pepper, sweet honey and malt. The finish holds the sweetness and citrus with a good length.

The exhibition area at Glen Ord Distillery shows how whisky used to be made. **85**

The Dalmore (Whyte & Mackay Ltd)

Region: Northern Highlands

Tel No: 01349 882362

Address: Alness, Ross-shire, IV17 0UT

Web Address: www.thedalmore.com

Nestling on the shores of the Cromarty Firth in Alness stands Dalmore Distillery. Owned for almost a century by the Clan Mackenzie, the stag motif on Dalmore bottles is taken from the Clan crest. The Mackenzies were friends with Charles Mackay and James Whyte of Glasgow and for many years Dalmore was sold to them for blending. In 1960 the family sold to Whyte & Mackay. Since then it has gone from strength to strength and in 2011 refurbished and re-launched the visitor centre, treating visitors to state-of-the-art tours.

Colour, Nose and Tasting Notes:
Dalmore 15 Year Old

Rich warm amber in colour, the nose is packed with rich Christmas-cake fruits, cinnamon and ginger spices plus soft aromas of orange and dark chocolate. The palate echoes the aromas, is medium bodied and has a lingering finish with spiced raisins, sticky ginger and cinnamon.

This beautifully preserved 1950s-vintage Commer lorry makes a fine sight outside **87** The Dalmore Distillery, complete with valuable load!

Glenmorangie (Louis Vuitton Moet Hennessy)

Region: Northern Highlands

Tel No: 01862 892477

Address: Tain, Ross-shire, IV19 1PZ

Web Address: www.glenmorangie.com

One of the oldest distilleries in production, there are records of distilling at Morangie farm as far back as the early 1700s, although it was in 1843 that a licence was acquired to produce whisky legally. Glenmorangie has famously tall stills, ensuring only the very lightest of vapours are distilled into spirit, making it one of the most popular single malts in Scotland. Glenmorangie also pioneered the use of a variety of wood finishes to create different expressions of the famous whisky. For example, the Quinta Ruban whisky is matured in American oak casks before being transferred to 'port pipes' from the Port and wine estates of Portugal.

Colour, Nose and Tasting Notes:
Glenmorangie 10 Year Old

Bright pale gold in colour, the nose has citrus fruits of mandarin combined with oak and floral notes. The palate has a sweetness of vanilla cream, citrus fruit, subtle honey and a little spice and almond. The finish is sweet, honeyed vanilla that lingers.

Glenmorangie Distillery. **89**

Clynelish (Diageo)

Region: Northern Highlands

Tel No: 01408 623000

Address: Brora, Sutherland, KW9 6LR

Web Address: www.discovering-distilleries.com

Clynelish was founded in 1819 by the Duke of Sutherland in the east-coast town of Brora. For many years it was only available privately, trade orders were refused! By 1933 the distillery had closed due to the Depression. It re-opened briefly between 1938 and 1941 when it closed again due to restrictions on the use of barley for making whisky during the Second World War. By the 1960s it had been refurbished and in 1967 a new distillery was built across the road and Clynelish moved. The original distillery was renamed Brora. This continued to produce whisky for a while but to a different recipe which was far more heavily peated. It has since closed and is now used for warehousing the Clynelish whisky.

Colour, Nose and Tasting Notes:
Clynelish 14 Year Old

Mid-gold in colour and a fragrant floral nose with hints of sea freshness, citrus elements and spices. The taste fills the mouth with smooth, rounded, slightly peaty flavours that lead on to hints of honey sweetness and Sherry.

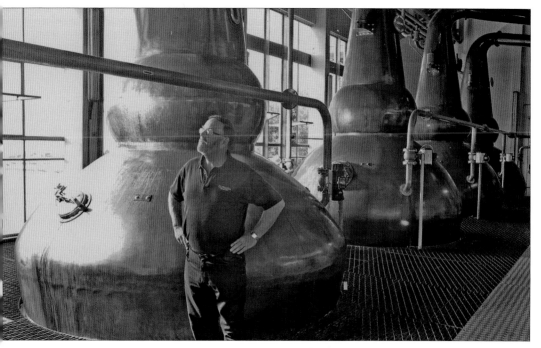

Checking the stills at Clynelish Distillery.

Pulteney (Inver House Distillers)

Region: Northern Highlands
Tel No: 01955 602371
Address: Huddart Street, Wick, Caithness, KW1 5BA
Web Address: www.oldpulteney.com

Old Pulteney Distillery is in the Caithness town of Wick. Known as the Maritime Malt, the distillery stands next to the harbour. Founded in 1826 by James Henderson, it is one of Scotland's most northerly mainland distilleries. Built at a time when the town was not very accessible by road, the whisky was made using barley brought in by boat. Wick became famous for its silver and gold exports, silver from the herring boom (it was the busiest herring port in Europe at one point) and gold from its whisky! Over time, the distillery has passed through the hands of various owners. It closed in the difficult times of 1930 but re-opened in 1947. Steeped in history, this is a distillery that deserves a visit.

Colour, Nose and Tasting Notes:
Old Pulteney 21 Year Old

Deep straw gold in colour, the nose is treated to aromas of orchard fruits, in particular pear with the merest hint of smoke. The fruitiness is held on the palate with some spice and creamy vanilla from the oak, with smoke wafting through. The finish is lingering and dry.

Old Pulteney 21 Year Old and the distillery sign.   93

Highland Park (Edrington)

Region: Highlands (Orkney)
Tel No: 01856 874619

Address: Holm Road, Kirkwall, Orkney, KW15 1SU
Web Address: www.highlandpark.co.uk

Highland Park Distillery is the most northern of Scotland's distilleries, located on Orkney. It has an interesting history since being started by Magnus Eunson, a whisky smuggler in the late 1700s. In 1816 John Robertson, a former excise man who had arrested Magnus Eunson, took over production. Since then it has been in several different companies' ownership, culminating in being bought by the Edrington group in 1999. It produces several ages of single malt, the most popular being the 12 Year Old. It is one of the few distilleries that malts some of its own barley and the whisky is predominantly matured in Sherry casks, some made from European oak and some from American oak, each giving different characteristics to the whisky.

Colour, Nose and Tasting Notes:
Highland Park Dark Origins

A rich, warm mahogany colour. On the nose, rich sherry overtones, nutmeg and cinnamon, tropical ripe bananas, nutty, toffee apple. On the palate it is sweet juicy raisins and sultanas, dark chocolate orange, some peat smoke. The finish is long and sweet with peat smoke.

Published 2015 by Ness Publishing, 47 Academy Street, Elgin, Moray, IV30 1LR. Reprinted 2016.
Phone 01343 549663 www.nesspublishing.co.uk
(First edition published 2012, second edition 2014)

Front cover: pagodas at Dalwhinnie Distillery; p.1: at The Glenlivet Distillery; p.4: portrait of George Smith; this page: at Glen Ord Distillery; back cover: Balvenie Distillery, Dufftown

For a list of websites and phone numbers please turn over >

Whisky Bars

EDINBURGH

Whiski Rooms, The Mound, 4 -7 North Bank Street, Edinburgh, EH1 2LP www.whiskirooms.co.uk
Whisky Shop (T) 0131 225 1532 Bar & Bistro (T) 0131 225 7224
Multi-award-winning whisky bar with a huge collection of Malt Whiskies and a really great atmosphere.

GLASGOW

Lismore, 206 Dumbarton Road, Glasgow, G11 6UW (T) 0141 576 0103
This Bar has an impressive selection of Malt Whisky and features traditional music sessions. You will mix with locals and international travellers visiting to appreciate this venue. The stained glass windows tell the story of the Highland Clearances.

Arisaig Bar and Restaurant, 1 Merchant Square, Candleriggs, Glasgow, G1 1LE (T) 0141 553 1010
www.arisaigrestaurant.co.uk

SPEYSIDE

The Highlander Inn, Craigellachie, Speyside, Banffshire, AB38 9SR (T) 01340 881446 www.whiskyinn.com
This Bar and Inn is in the centre of Speyside and has become internationally known by whisky lovers from all over the world. Expertly run with passion and dedication, it even has its own bottling unique to the Inn.

The Mash Tun, 8 Broomfield Square, Aberlour, Speyside, AB38 9QP (T) 01340 881771 www.mashtun-aberlour.com
The Mash Tun is located in the heart of Aberlour close to the old railway station and Speyside Way, so if you are walking this is an ideal resting point where you can taste a fabulous collection of Glenfarclas Malts.

Knockomie Hotel, Grantown Road, Forres, Moray, IV36 2SG (T) 01309 673146 www.knockomie.co.uk
Pleasant Inn, located on A940 just south of Forres with an extensive collection of Malts.

The Drouthy Cobbler , 48a High Street, Elgin, IV30 1BU 01343 596000 www.thedrouthycobbler.co.uk